the art of A. RAMACHANDRAN

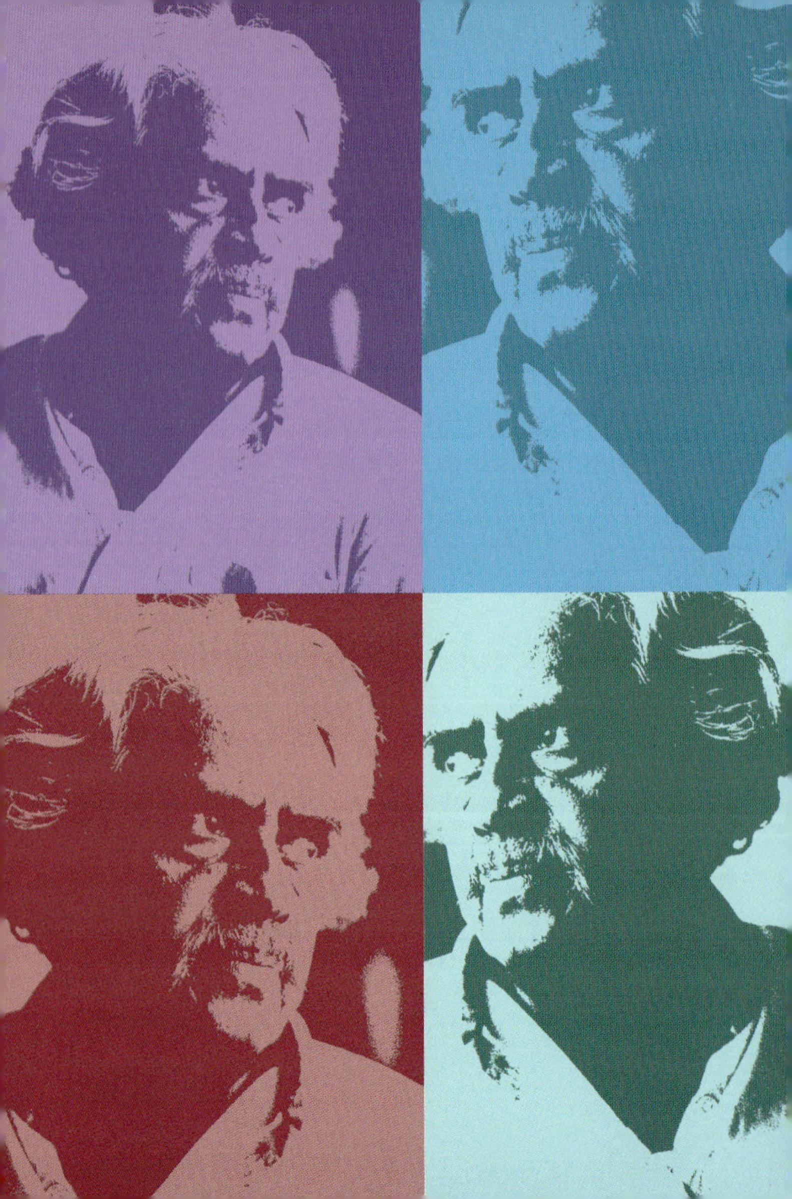

the art of A. RAMACHANDRAN

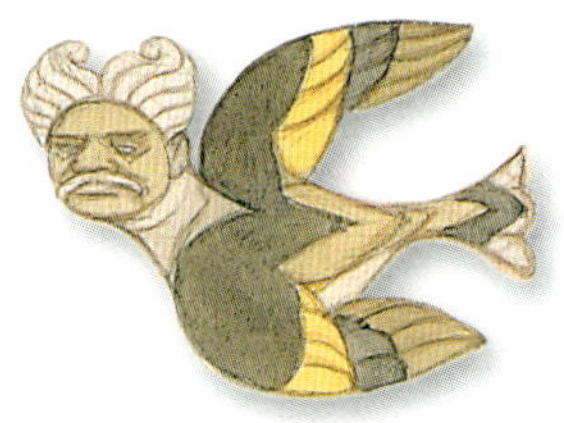

Ella Datta

Lustre Press
Roli Books

A. Ramachandran's paintings are enigmatic. The sensuous environment – men, women, birds, insects, trees, flowers – that he recreates on canvas or on paper are not simple records of natural beauty meant to please the eye. Instead, they are layered with references to artistic expressions of past ages, mythology and a very personal world view.

Born in Kerala in 1935, Achutan Nair Ramachandran's first attempts with paint and brush occurred when he was a little boy.

One day when alone at home, he thought of improving an oil portrait hanging on a wall. His efforts were not taken kindly by his family. Soon, however, they realised his artistic inclinations. Ramachandran was admitted to a private art school as a boy of 11 or so. He was taught to draw the human figure in the academic realist style that was common in Kerala because of Raja Ravi Varma's overarching influence.

It did not take very long for Ramachandran to turn away from these early art lessons. He says, 'I always revolted against what is close to life. Creativity, after all, is not restricted to logic. I preferred to fantasise.'

This ability was fed by many external stimuli, the most significant being the impressions of the Krishnaswamy temple at Attingal, a small town.

He wrote, 'Whenever my mother took me around the *garbha griha* for the customary perambulation . . . I used to stare at the *garbha griha* walls with immense curiosity. In the dimly lit courtyard, the walls looked like a rich tapestry of colour patches'.

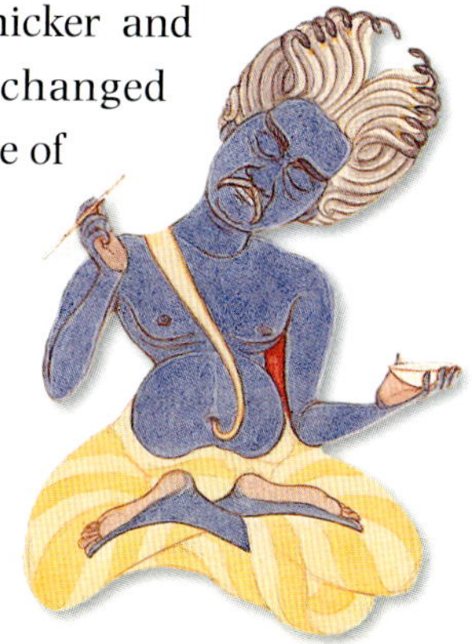

Ramachandran had planned to go to the Madras College of Art because of his acquaintance with K.C.S. Panicker and his works. But his plans changed suddenly when he saw a picture of Ramkinkar's 'Santhal Family'. It made a deep impression on him and he was determined to study under Ramkinkar in Santiniketan. 'Going to Santiniketan was a sheer accident,' says Ramachandran. Some may say Santiniketan was the artist's destiny.

In 1957, with little money in his pocket and a letter of introduction, young Ramachandran left for Santiniketan. The first year went badly. Ramkinkar showed no interest in his work. Later, however, Ramachandran became very close to him. The closeness was depicted in Ramachandran's famous totemic bronze sculpture, 'Iconic Self-portrait with Ramkinkar'.

Ramachandran's art training began with sketching the Santhal villages to which he was initiated by painter Kiran Sinha. It was in one of these village huts that Ramachandran used to do oils secretly and keep the material hidden in the hayloft. At the time oil as a medium was a big No-No in Santiniketan.

Completing his diploma in fine arts and crafts from Kala Bhavan, Visva Bharati, in 1961, for the next four years, Ramachandran did post-graduate research on his beloved Kerala murals for a doctoral thesis with Visva Bharati. In 1964, he relocated to Delhi at the invitation of

Virendra Kumar Jain of Kumar Art Gallery. In 1965, he joined the Jamia Milia University as a lecturer of art education. Two years later, he married Tan Chameli, a beautiful Chinese girl whom he met in Santiniketan and who had also studied at Kala Bhavan.

By this time, he was well entrenched in the imagination of Indian viewers for his huge, haunting paintings. They were re-enactments of the themes of victims and oppressors, of hunters and prey. The figuration was classically expressionistic.

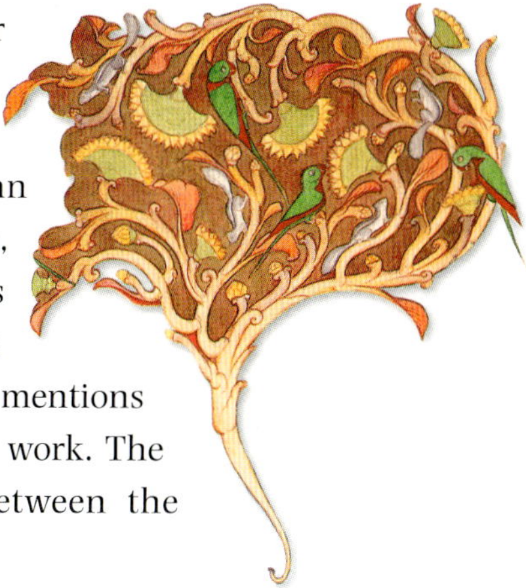

But Ramachandran says, 'I was not a follower of the European expressionism'. Instead, the Mexican muralists like Rivera, Orozco and Siqueiros inspired him greatly. Ramachandran often mentions a contradiction in his work. The contradiction lies 'between the logic of the external world and one's own internal visualisation'. Throughout his evolving visual language, this contradiction played a formative role.

Coming from Kerala, a strong political consciousness was a part of his mindset during the early period of his works. At the time, he says, 'I was spurred by incidents'.

One such incident of animal sacrifice during a Kali puja celebration prompted him to paint 'Kali Puja' in 1962 in encaustic, where pigments are mixed with wax.

Some 10 years later, he painted a second version of 'Kali Puja' after a visit to Santiniketan in 1971. He was unprepared for the political turbulence that gripped West Bengal – the Naxalite uprising. Recalls Ramachandra, 'There was an air of fear everywhere, terror in the hearts of the people.' The 'Kali Puja' (1972) was a huge triptych done in oil. The distorted headless figures in contorted stances, menacing weapons, sacrificial stands, brilliant colours, all combine to create an awesome comment on the state of violence.

Ramachandran maintains, 'Art is a very personal statement. It is the artist's response to the life around. A work of art causes a flicker, a moment where one gets an aesthetic experience akin to spiritual experience.' Since the '80s, Ramachandran has been seeking to break the limits of the mundane and creating a mystical experience. He has used every skill in his command – sharply drawn supple, sinuous lines, a luminous colour palette, deft control over forms, a vast bank of references from past visual traditions. He has captured the many moods of the natural world with its lush vegetation, exuberant animals, birds and insects, people full of vitality.

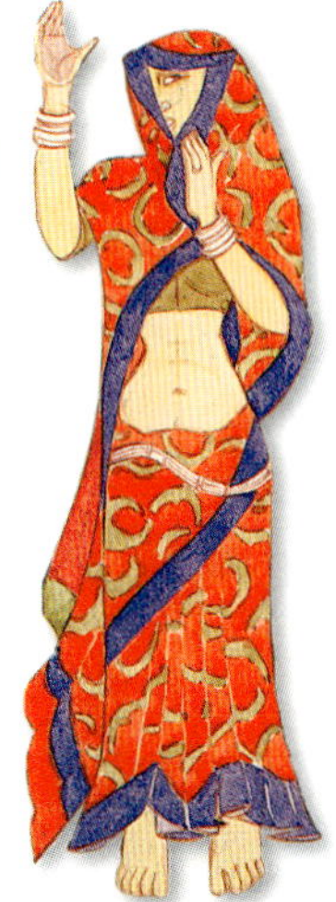

The change from the angst-ridden images to an idyllic mindscape did not come suddenly. From the early '70s, Ramachandran had been visiting distant tribal areas around Udaipur

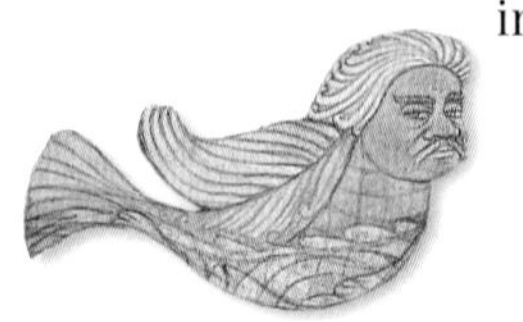

in Rajasthan. He says, 'I have had two intense love affairs. One is with Chameli, the other with Rajasthan.'

After the nuclear explosion in Pokhran in 1974, Ramachandran worked on a major series of paintings called 'Nuclear Ragini'. A couple of obvious changes, influenced by Rajasthan, occurred about this time.

For the first time, draped Rajasthani women began to appear in his work. As a take-off from this point, the artist used an interesting device which heightened the sense of mystery – an opening in the head covering of women which reveals only one eye through the triangular space.

The second development that took place was the use of direct quotes from earlier Indian painting traditions such as the Rajasthani miniatures. A woman looking at a mirror from a Kota miniature appeared in a painting. Only, instead of her reflection, she saw a skull, a reference to the nuclear destruction. It was

Ramachandran's acerbic wit which gave a vitriolic twist to a romantic motif in art.

It took another political event in 1984 – the horrific anti-Sikh riots following the assassination of Mrs Indira Gandhi – that made Ramachandran turn away from making direct political comments in his painting. The sight of such extreme human misery made him determined not to sublimate such raw experience of agony into art. Instead, he turned towards a more timeless contemplation of the natural world. He zeroed in on the tribal village landscapes near Udaipur – Baneshwar and Nagda – and the lives of the tribals, the Bhils and Gaudia Lohars, which gave him a fresh perspective with their vitality.

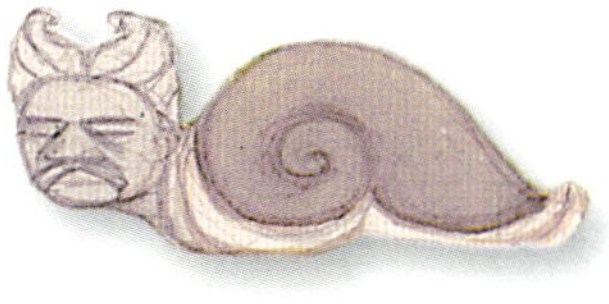

During the '70s and early '80s, Ramachandran's exposure to the Rajasthani miniature traditions led him to create three sets of miniatures. Brilliant in their execution, the miniatures carry the stamp of the artist's wit, black humour and irony, once again with an element of contradiction. Romanticism is tempered with irony, while a lofty sentiment is given an earthy perspective.

It was also during this period that Ramachandran won national and international acclaim as a writer, illustrator and book designer of children's books, particularly in Japan.

But this was also a period of personal upheavals. Ramachandran had major health problems. The most serious of these was an eye affliction gravely affecting his vision. This is a desperate nightmare for an artist. Ramachandran, however, successfully overcame the physical challenge, and by the early '80s, he had worked out a new idiom of expression.

He dismisses the idea of sudden change. 'It was a slow logical process. I was looking for a redefinition of visual language.' He set about deconstructing the elements of tradition to devise an idiom that would recreate living images. He thanks the discipline of his

Santiniketan training and the teachings of his mentors for his ability to do this.

At a time when the word tradition was being critiqued, he grappled with it to give it a fresh context. Consider the new iconography of women that he presented. The Hannas, Savitas, Ratnis in his work are not conventional archetypes of female representation. These women with their high cheekbones, flattened noses, thick lips and sensuous bodies present an alternative iconographic experience that is almost a challenge. It is the same with his trees and flowers.

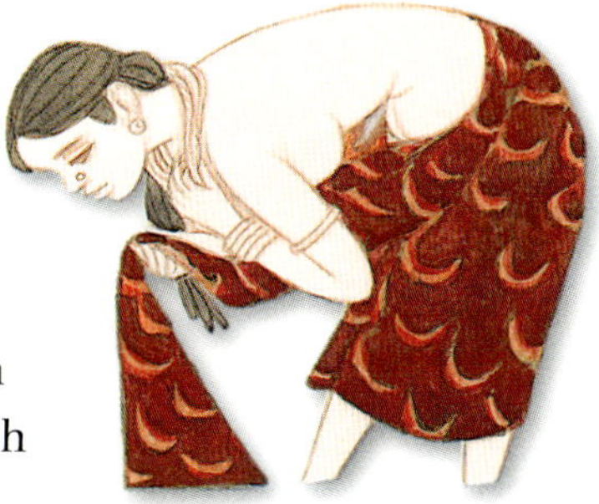

Consider also the many ways that he introduces elements of surprise in the idyllic images that he creates. The gramophone – a symbol of modern technology – in a mythical / pastoral setting, or the self-portrait of the artist as a bee or a snail gives a fresh perspective to the image. Ramachandran sets a teasing relationship between the viewer, the artist and the canvas.

Writing in the Prologue of *Ramachandran: Icons of the Raw Earth* by Rupika Chawla, Ramachandran said, 'I realised that the most significant component of our visual language was line and line alone. Since the usage of line in Indian art was of a distinctive nature unlike the calligraphic line of Chinese art, decorativeness was inevitable. Just as our architecture, sculpture, music and dance are filled with embellishment, the picture space is animated by the diction of the lines.'

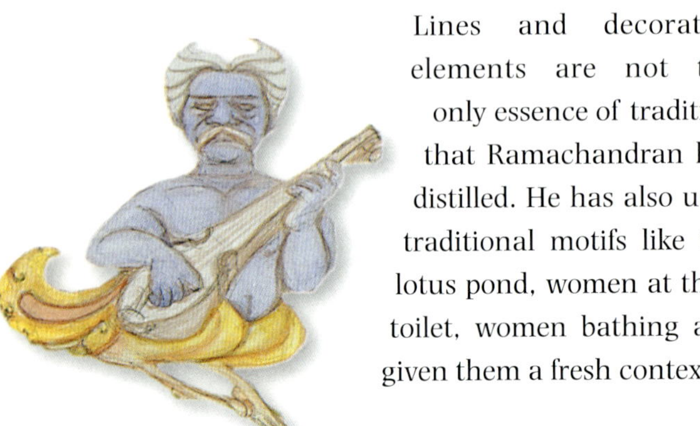

Lines and decorative elements are not the only essence of tradition that Ramachandran has distilled. He has also used traditional motifs like the lotus pond, women at their toilet, women bathing and given them a fresh context.

In 1986, he showed the installation Yayati, composed of large paintings and bronze sculptures. To the myth of a king afraid to lose his youthful vigour, Ramachandran wove strands like the daily life of the Gaudia Lohars and his own personal emotions. He refers to the picturisation of the traditional myth 'as an old man's vision of a sensuous world slipping away from him'.

The result was a dazzling play of pliant, voluptuous forms and intense colours. But it is impossible for a viewer to impose a narrative on so complexly constructed an imagery. The artist says, 'There is no narrative. I am not an illustrator and I refuse to allow anybody to read my paintings.'

Yayati was followed by Urvashi and Pururavas which in turn was followed by 'Reality in Search of a Myth'. If Yayati comprised highly finished, voluptuous forms reminiscent of Kerala murals and Ajanta, then the Urvashi series recalled the sinuous, elongated forms and colourings of Alchi and early Gujarat miniatures. The palette was imbued with a diffused glow.

Referring to the Urvashi series, the artist says that she is not just a mythical creature: 'She is also an idealised notion of my art.' Ramachandran says that all his life he has searched for the right formal treatment for his aesthetic preoccupations.

Ramachandran is involved with the idea of colour and is attracted to its 'extraordinary sensuousness'. Ramachandran's articulations in sculpture also need special mention. The artist has created murals including the one at Gandhi Darshan in Delhi. He has also tried his hand at stamp design and ceramics.

Painter and sculptor, Ramachandran is eternally in search of a new language to create an experience beyond life which nevertheless springs from a basis of reality.

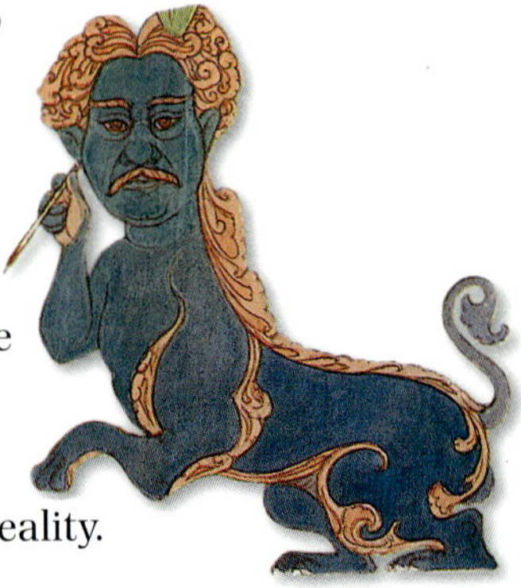

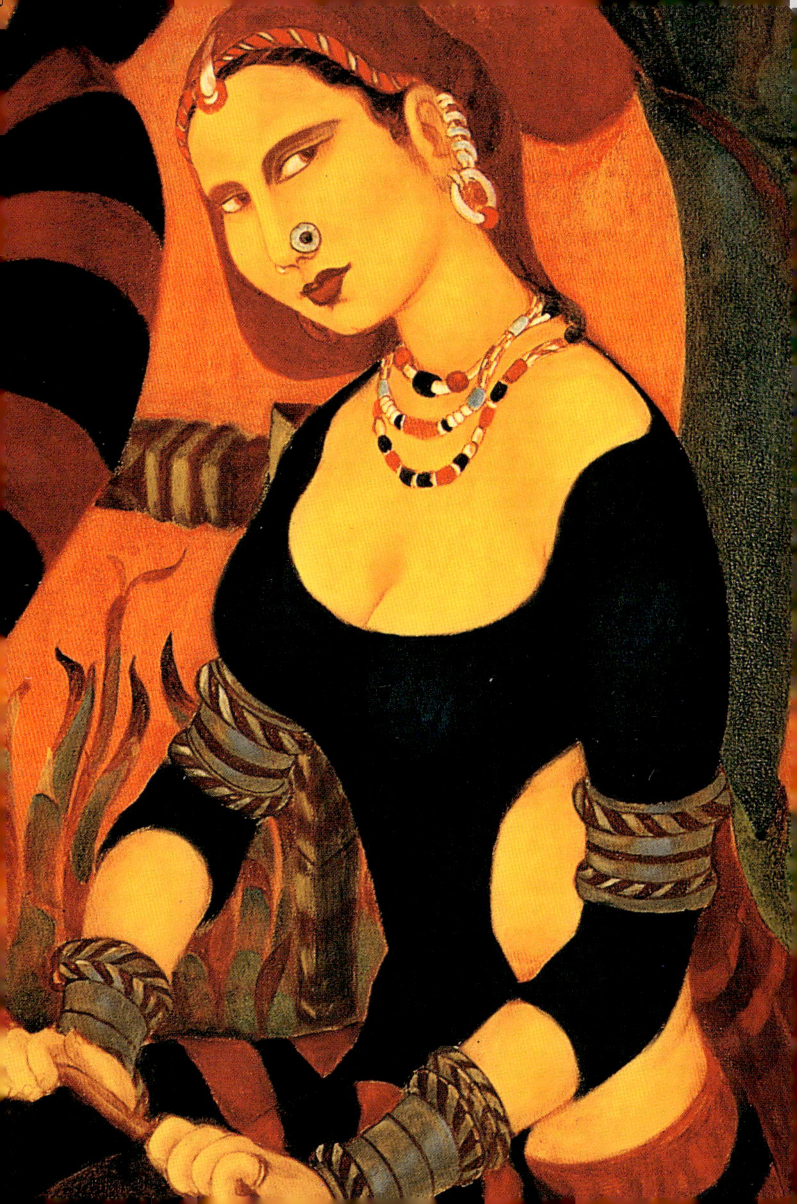

■ Detail from Yayati

This was the first series of paintings when Ramachandran turned away from expressionism and chose a language which was not a copy of tradition but a continuation of idiom and style. The highly finished muralistic paintings are reminiscent of Kerala murals and Ajanta. Ramachandran captures the vibrant activities of Gaudia Lohars in this myth of an old man's fantasies of a sensuous world. 6' x 8', oil on canvas, 1982-86.

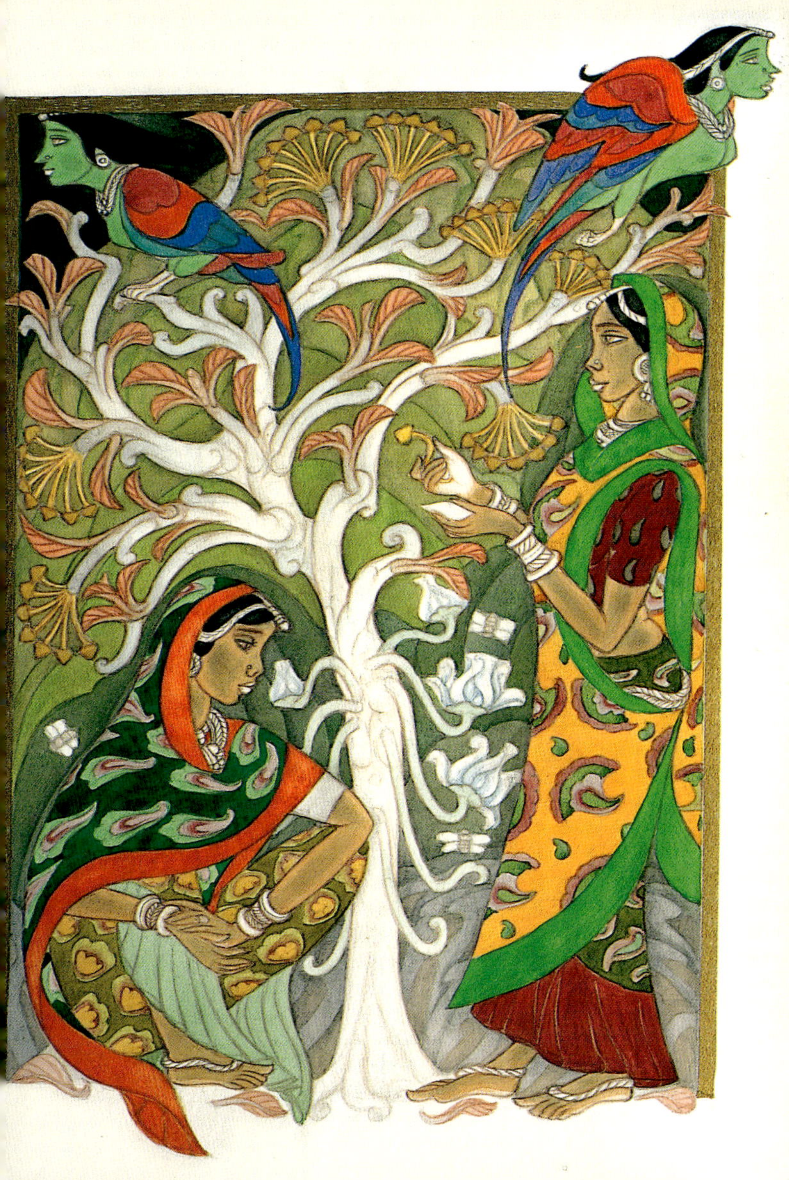

■ *Mahua* tree in blossom

The mahua *tree is a favourite botanical specimen in Ramachandran's repertoire, along with* palash, aparajita, kanchan, *and a few others. The painter uses the* mahua *tree as a symbol of artistic creativity. Just as the potent juice of the* mahua *fruit gives the drinker a heady experience, so also the artist's creativity spurs him to fantasise his own painted world. Here two women in their brightly coloured clothes are gathered in front of a flowering* mahua *tree. The flaming flowers create a contrast with the curving, curling white branches of the tree. Perched on top are two brightly coloured bird-women who balance the colourful clothes of the two women on the ground.* 11.5" x 15.5", watercolour, 1997.

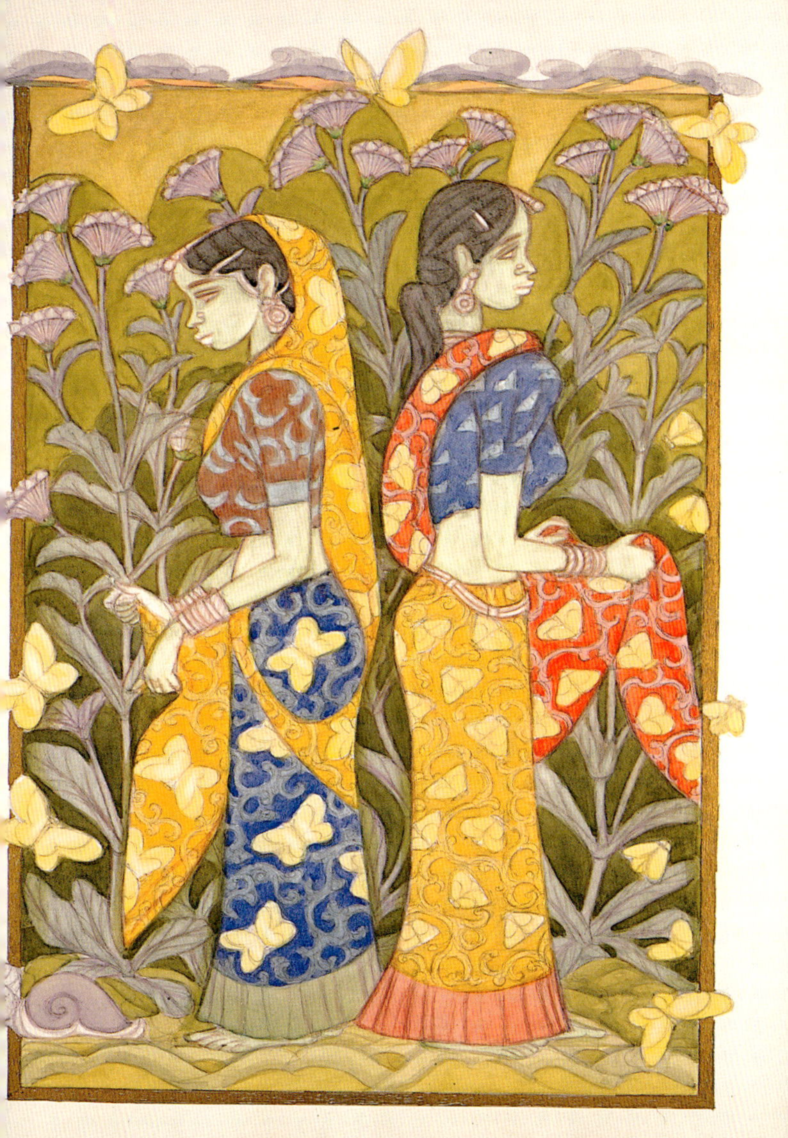

■ Girls and the insects

The artist captures a joyous landscape. Two girls stand amid a thick growth of flowering plants. Numerous butterflies flit about lifting the scene with great elan. The butterflies are synonymous with the patterns on the girls' skirts. The artist as a tiny snail observes the scene from the lower left hand corner of the painting. It is worth seeing the way that colour fields are created. Note the same saturated blue in one girl's skirt and in another girl's choli. 11.5" x 15.5", watercolour, 1997.

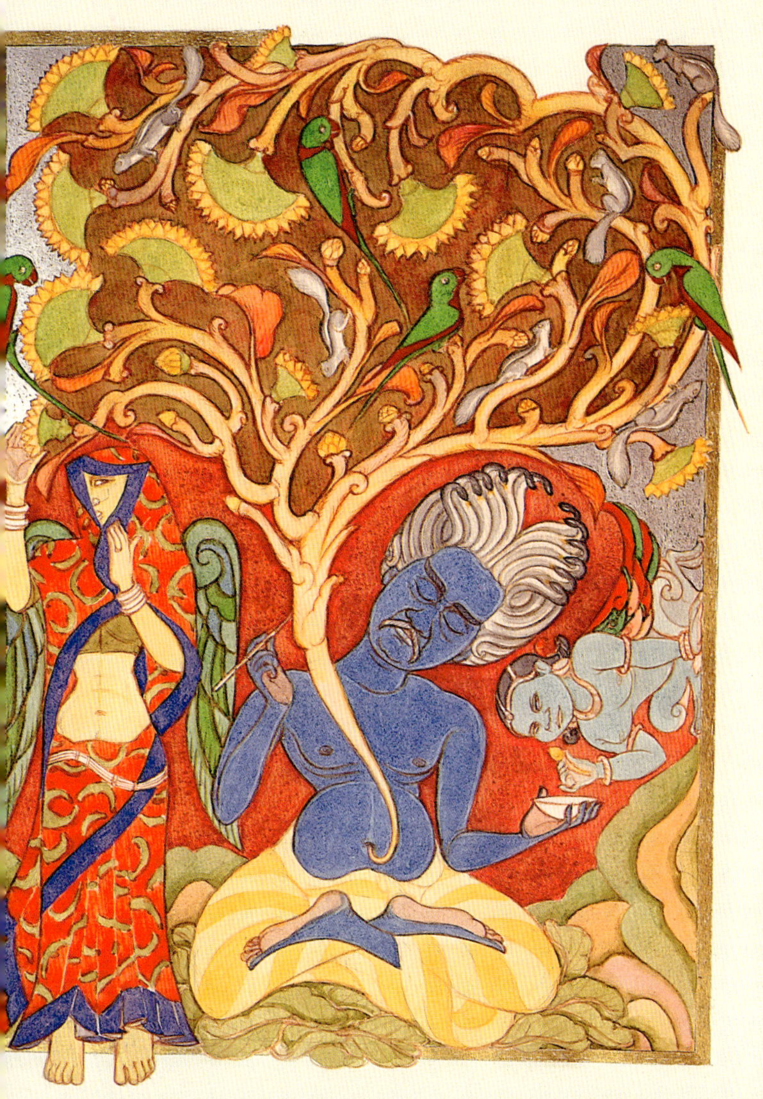

■ Iconic self-portrait with umbilical *mahua* tree

The watercolour comes from the early stages of Ramachandran's mythification of his encounter with the tribals of Rajasthan. This is a wonderful depiction of the artist as the creator. Like the myth of Brahma emerging on a lotus from Vishnu's navel, the mahua *tree rises from the umbilical chord of the artist. The blossoming tree has an intoxicating fruit. There is an ambiguity about the artist's illusion as a creator. Is it the heady fruit extract that adds to the illusion or is it the artist's own ability with brush and bowl of paint that creates a whole world from his fantasies? The winged creature on one side and Ekanayani, an iconic representation of a woman with her head covered, adds to the sense of an illusory landscape.* 11.5" x 15.5", watercolour, 1993.

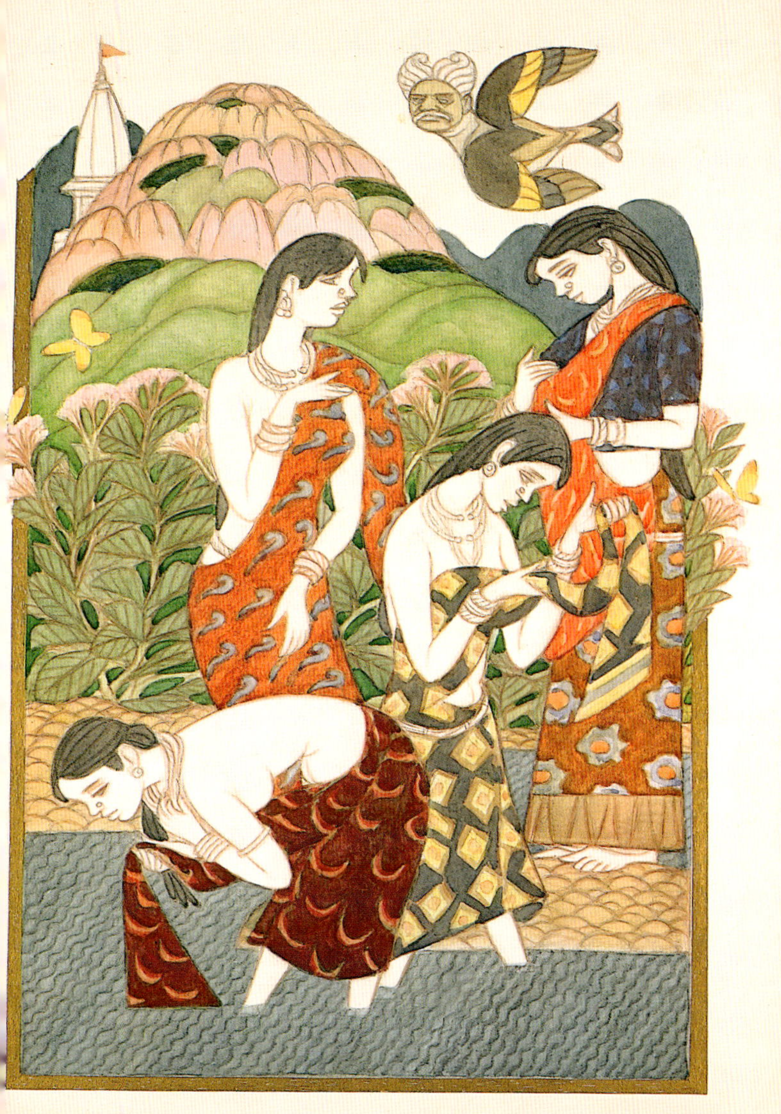

■ Bathers at Baneswar *mela*

Baneshwar, at some distance from Udaipur, has often figured in Ramachandran's paintings. There is a Shiva temple on a small hillock which dominates the scene. On the first full moon after mid-February, there is a mela *or fair held on the grounds below the temple. All the tribal villages in the neighbourhood come to celebrate the auspicious occasion. Here four women are bathing in the open-air tank. In the background, the white* shikhara *of the temple can be glimpsed. In a teasing mood, the artist turns himself into a bird looking on at the scene.*

Ramachandran turns the whole notion of the male gaze on its head by becoming a part of the scene himself where the focus is not just on the beauty of the female form but on the whole idyllic scene. 11.5" x 15.5", watercolour, 1997.

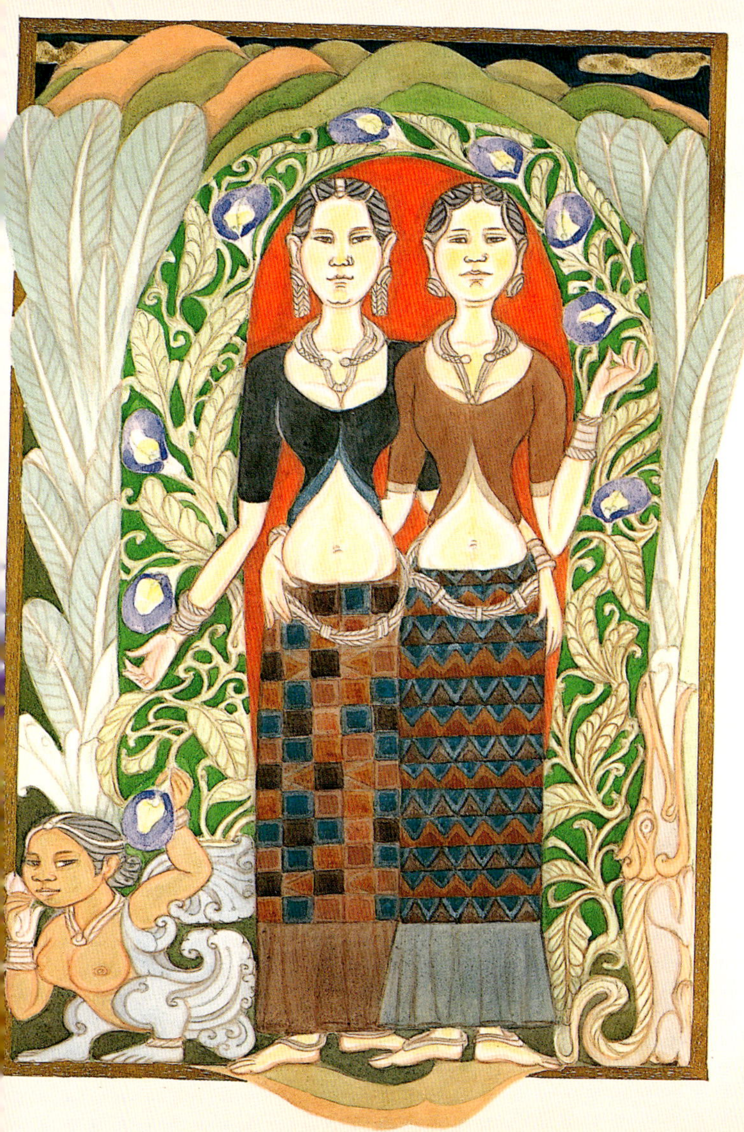

■ Girls with *aparajita* flowers

Two girls stand frontally like icons with arms clasping each other. They are framed by lush vegetation. The flowering aparajita *framing them has many associations. The flowers are considered to be the flowers linked with the mother goddess. The curiously shaped, velvety blue flowers themselves have connotations of sexuality. The* aparajita, *like the lotus, is a favourite decorative floral element for the painter. The women in the dark blue and red patterned skirts evoke the colour and texture of the flowers. The little bird-woman in the lower left of the frame helps to accentuate the fantasy element. The erotic overtones reflect the creative energy of the natural world.* 11.5" x 15.5", watercolour, 1996.

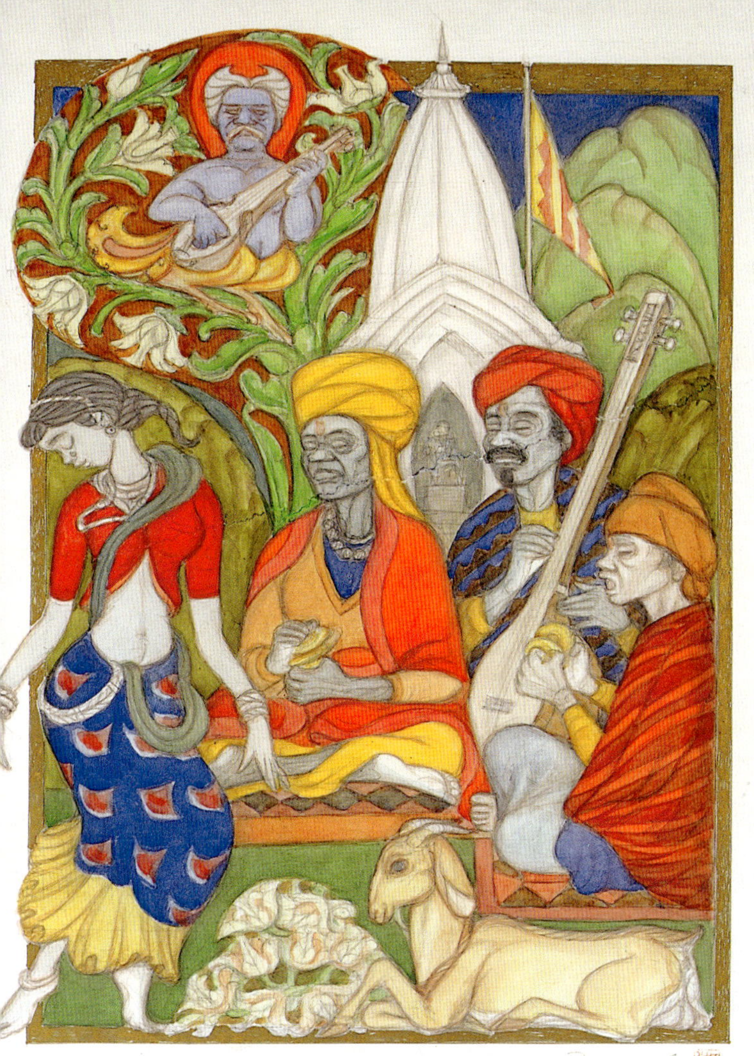

■ In praise of Ramdev

This little village shrine nestling amid the hill forms a typical setting for a Ramachandran painting. There is a young girl dancing accompanied by a group of village musicians. A goat in the foreground counterpoints the flowing movements of the dancer. The artist playing a folk instrument has sublimated himself into a deity who looks down on the devotional scene taking place below. The movements of the girl dancing resemble the creeping, twining flowering plant framing the artist. The diverse forms and colours meld into a wonderful mosaic. 11.5" x 15.5", watercolour, 1997.

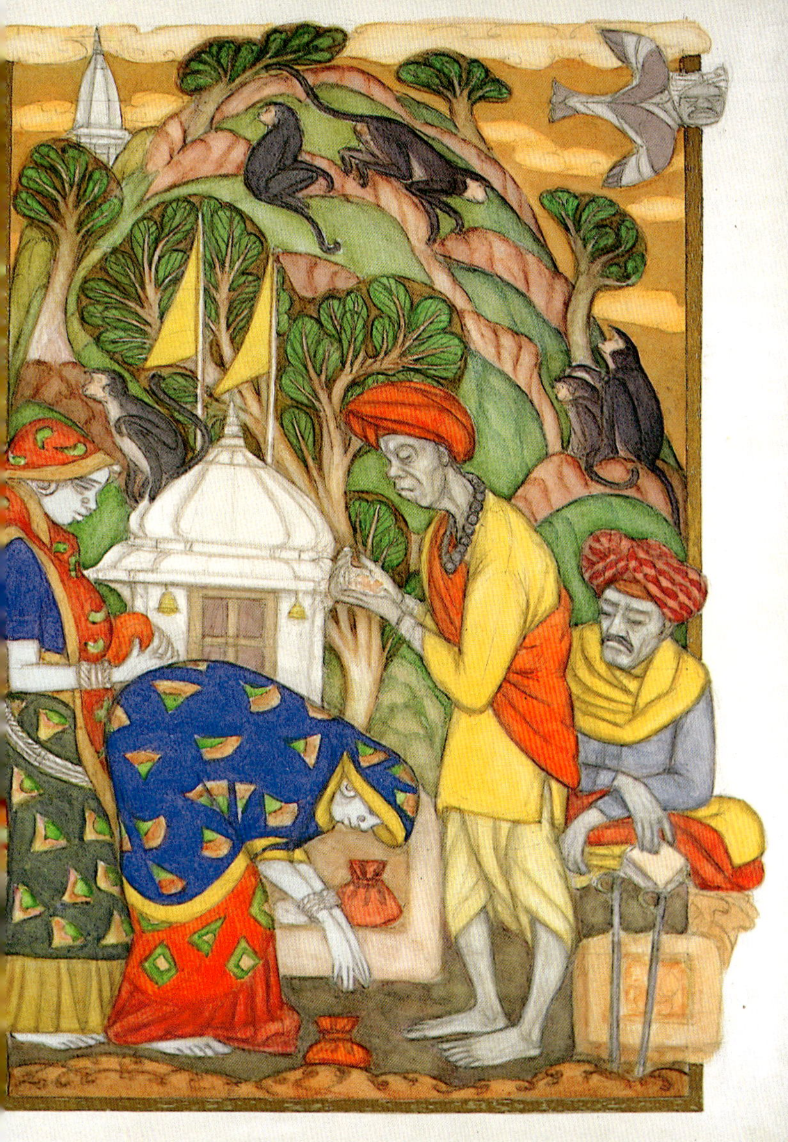

■ The devotees of Dhowraji

Dhowraji is a bhopa *– a religious leader of his village. He is a worshipper of the tribal deity Ramdev. There is no contradiction in his life even though he is also a member of the Communist Party coming into the capital to participate in May Day processions. As a* bhopa*, in this tranquil scene before a village shrine, he receives the obeisance of two young women. In the distance can be seen the* shikhara *of the Baneshwar temple. The scene is a part of the natural universe of the Bhils – temples, shrines, hills, trees, cavorting monkeys. On the upper right-hand corner Ramachandran looks on at the scene as a bird.* 11.5" x 15.5", watercolour, 1997.

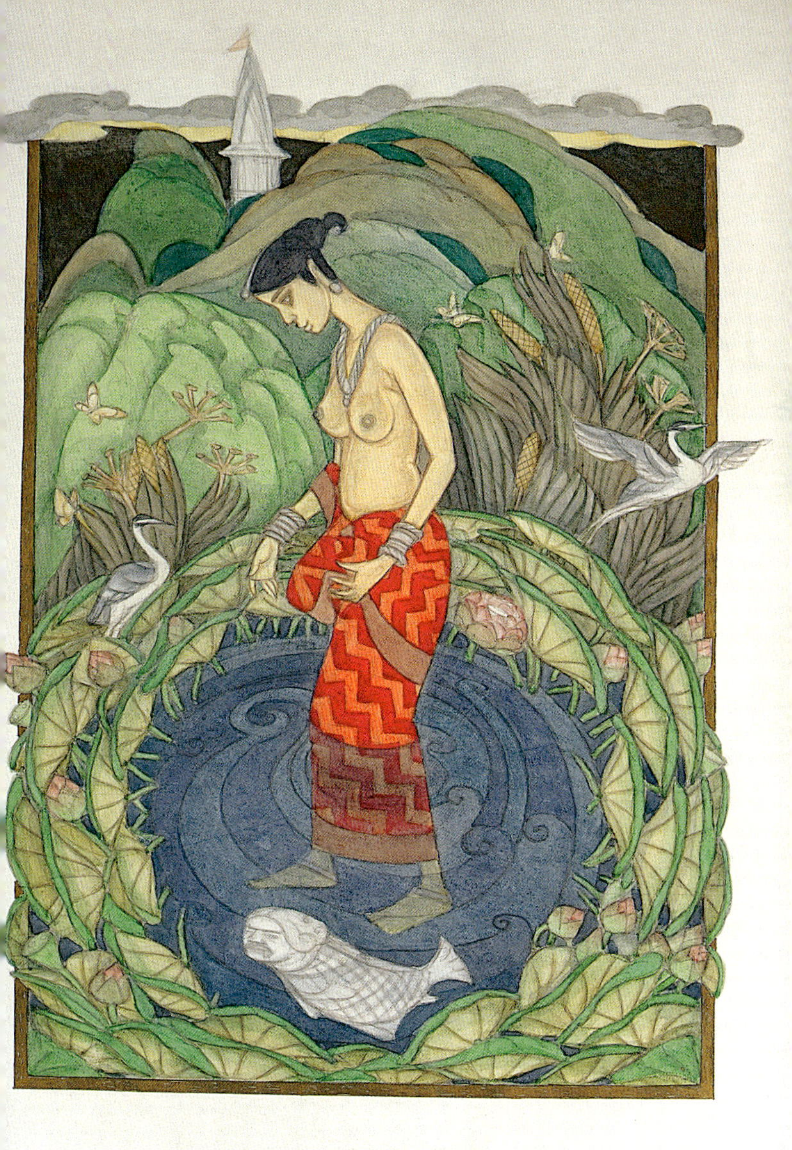

■ Matsyavatar at Nagda

Ramachandran turns the myth of Matsyavatar (Vishnu's incarnation as a fish to uphold the world) to create his own mythic landscape. His favourite elements are all there: the lotus pond, the water birds, the temple shikhara *rising beyond the hills. The young girl standing unrobed and ready for a dip in the pool of water is being watched by the artist turned into a fish. The colours in this very private scene have been applied with an exquisite precision.* 11.5" x 15.5". watercolour, 1997.

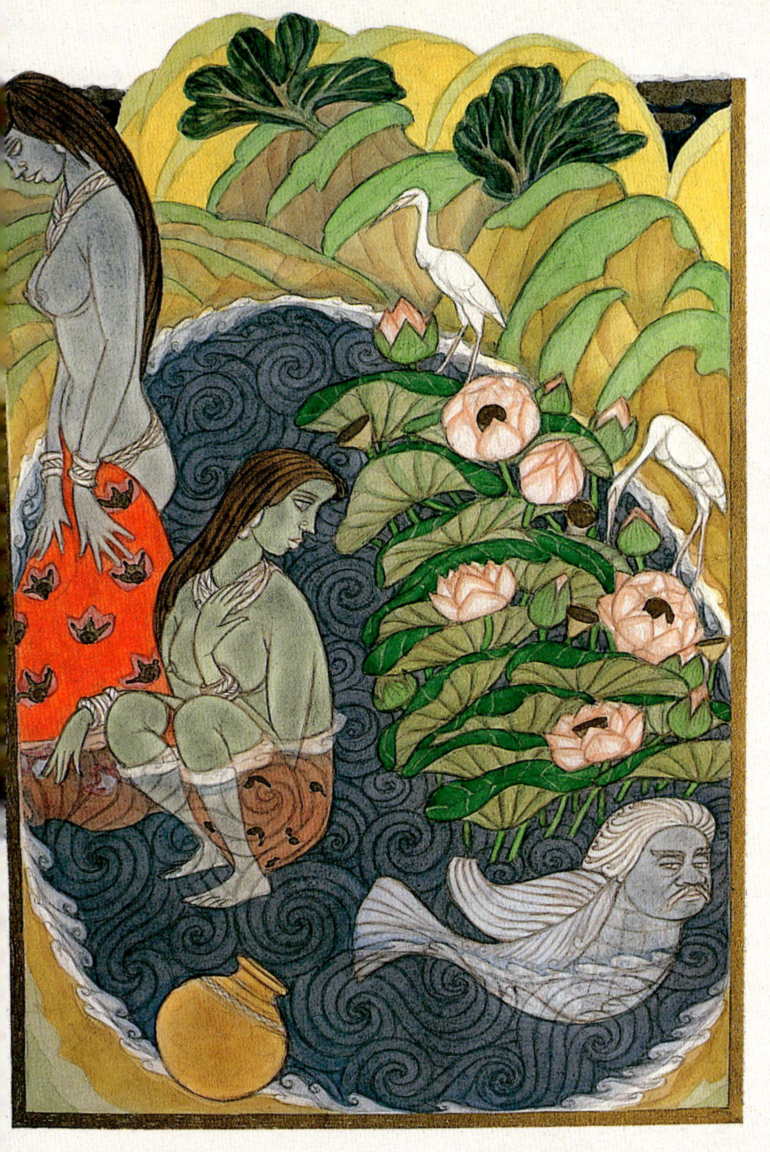

■ Matsyavatar at Nagda II

Just as Vishnu appeared in several incarnations to save the world in times of calamity, so also artist Ramachandran records an idyllic world that is threatened with destruction as a fallout of urbanisation and encroaching technology.

Two girls are bathing in a secluded pool framed by green hills and trees. A clump of lotus flowers bloom on one side. The two saras *birds may have references to miniature paintings. But the artist does not forget that in Indian tradition the bird also symbolises wisdom. The artist contemplates the scene as a fish lazily swimming in the pool.* 11.5" x 15.5", watercolour, 1996.

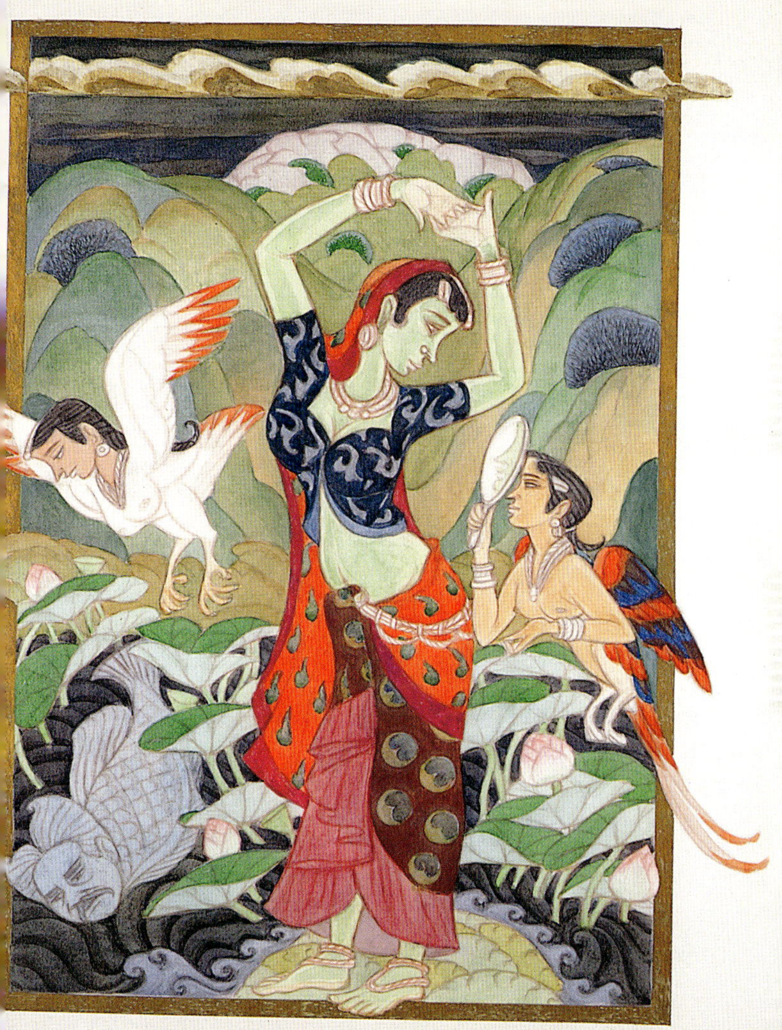

■ Matsyavatar

The painting has a direct reference to the nayikas *of the Rajasthani miniatures. Only her face does not have the sharp features of the Rajasthani miniatures. The ornaments are also of the kind that tribal girls wear. The artist as a fish is watching a young girl in a dance pose. She is lost to the world watching herself in the mirror held by a winged creature. There is another winged creature standing by. The stylisation of the hills and the sky, as treated in miniatures, is noteworthy.* 11.5" x 15.5", watercolour, 1996.

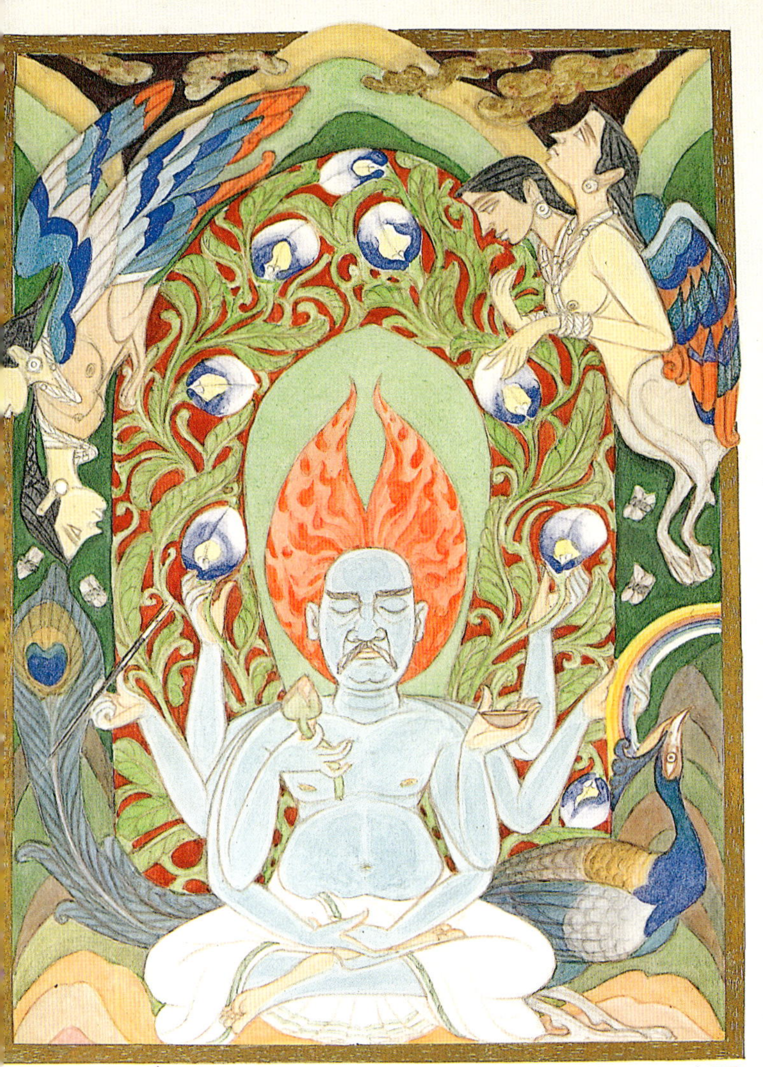

■ Self-portrait of artist as creator

Just as the artist as observer and participant obssesses him, so also does the concept of the artist as creator. Here Ramachandran with his flaming hair, is seen as an eight-armed seated deity. He has a seated peacock behind him. A creeper of velvety blue aparajita *flowers with strong erotic associations in the shape of its flowers acts as a frame of the stele behind him. The winged creatures add to the richness of this magical creation.* 11.5" x 15.5", watercolour, 1996.

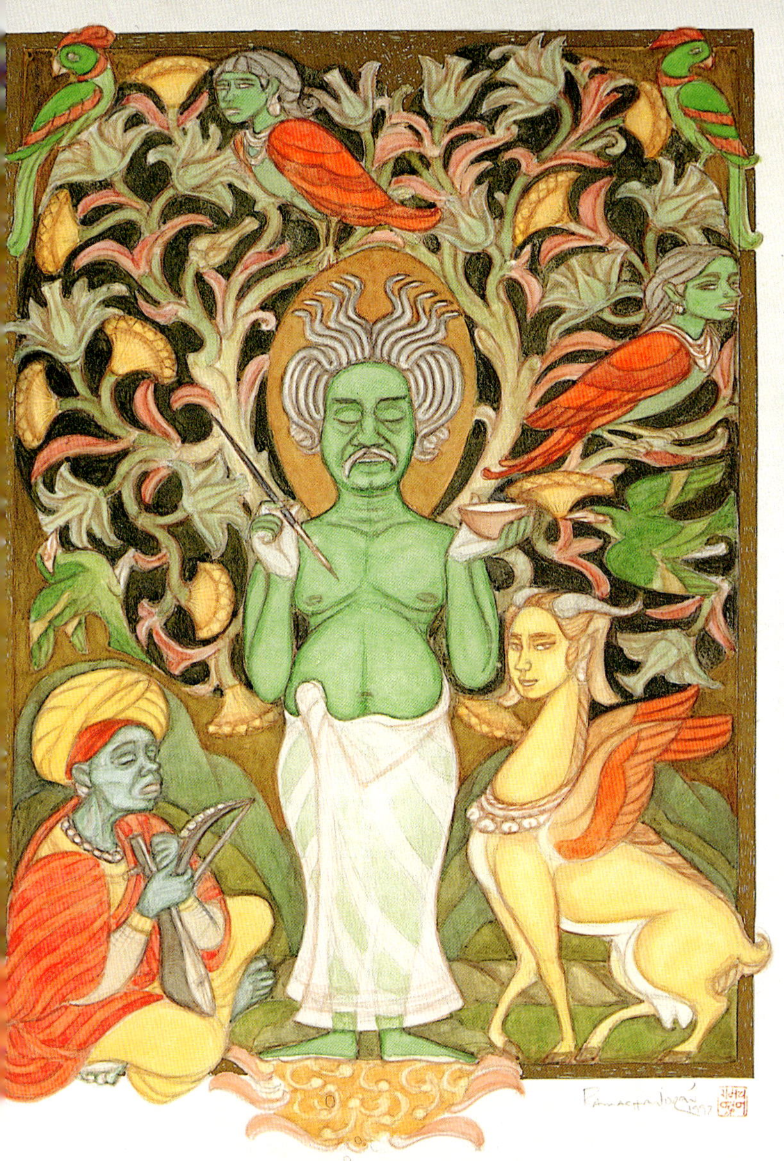

■ In praise of Ramdev II

Here the artist Ramachandran as the icon Ramdev, a popular tribal deity, is the central figure. He creates his own universe with his brush and bowl of paint. There is abundant vegetation around him springing up strong and sinuous and filling the background. Birds and bird-women fill the flowering branches. A seated villager sings in praise of the artist's creation while a mythical beast – half-woman, half-winged animal – sits elegantly in front. 11.5" x 15.5", watercolour, 1997.

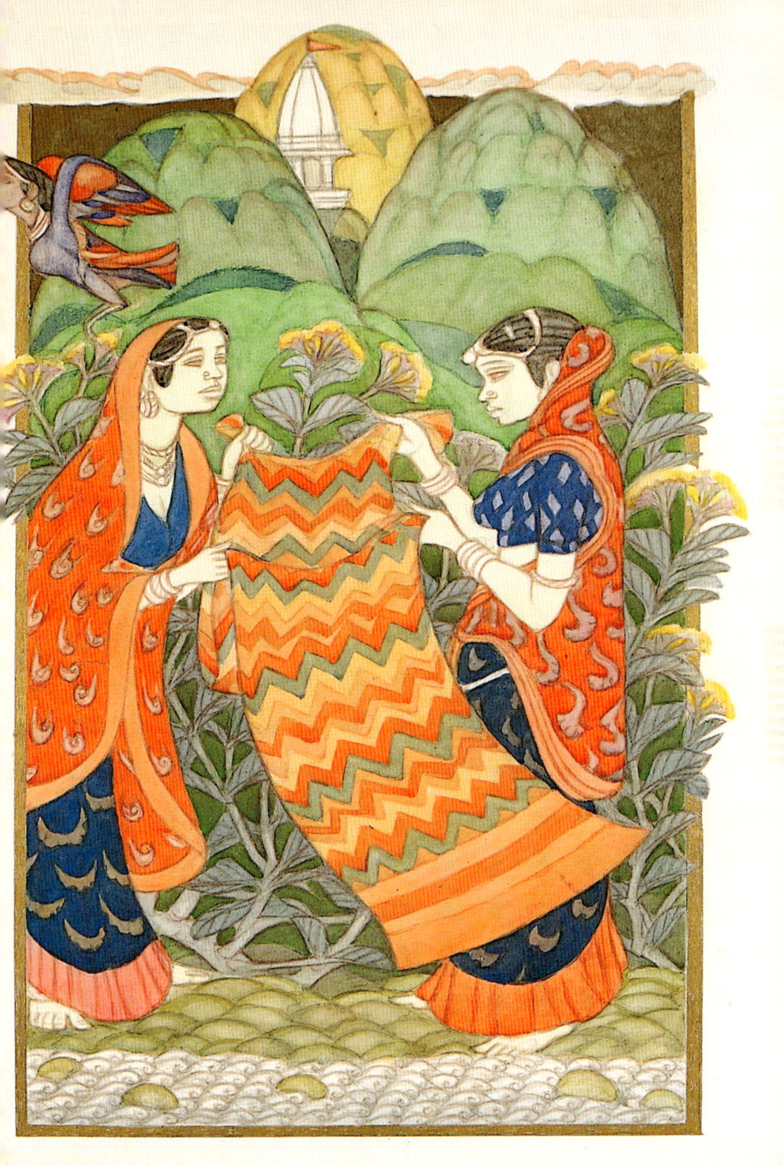

■ Women drying a cloth at Baneshwar

A beautiful example of how Ramachandran transforms a real-life scene into a total visual experience of colours, lines and forms. The presence of the winged woman introduces a touch of fantasy. The way the artist breaks out of the rectangular frame of the painting is worth observing. 11.5" x 15.5", watercolour, 1997.

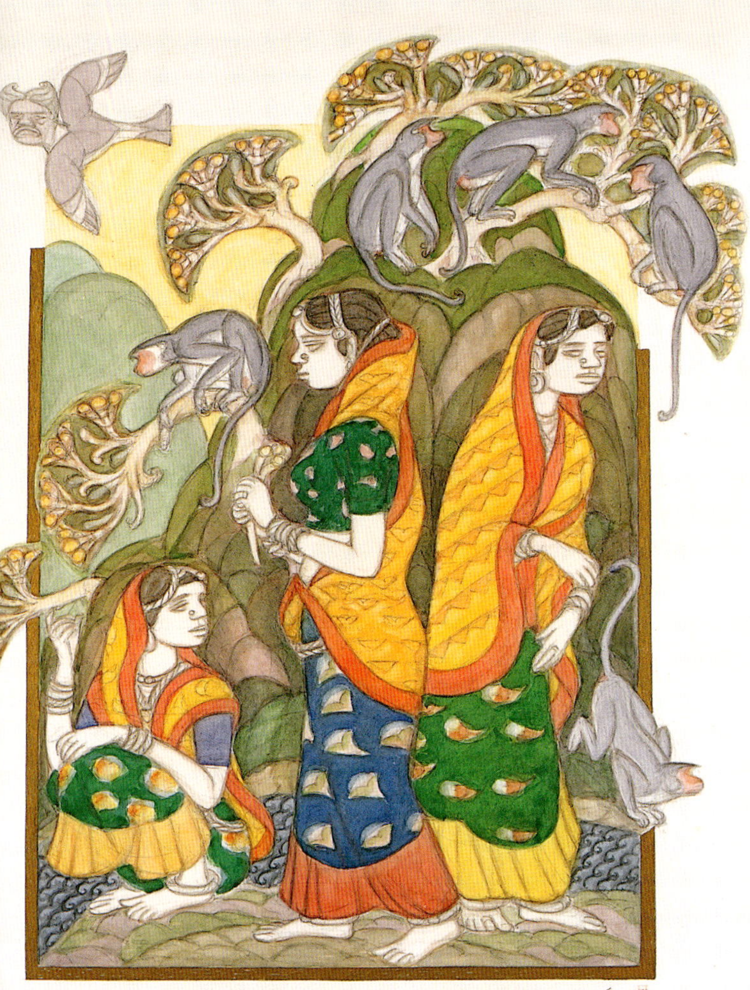

■ Resting on the way to Baneshwar

A group of three girls refresh themselves while undertaking the long trek to the Baneshwar mela. *In the background, the monkeys frolic in the thick vegetation. The flowering tree and a narrow sliver of flowing water add to a mythic setting. Ramachandran as a grey bird, watches the scene from the sky. The brilliant colours of the girls' clothes stand out against the muted greys of the monkeys and the subtle colours of the flowering tree. The blue sliver of flowing water knits the whole scene together.* 11.5" x 15.5", watercolour, 1997.

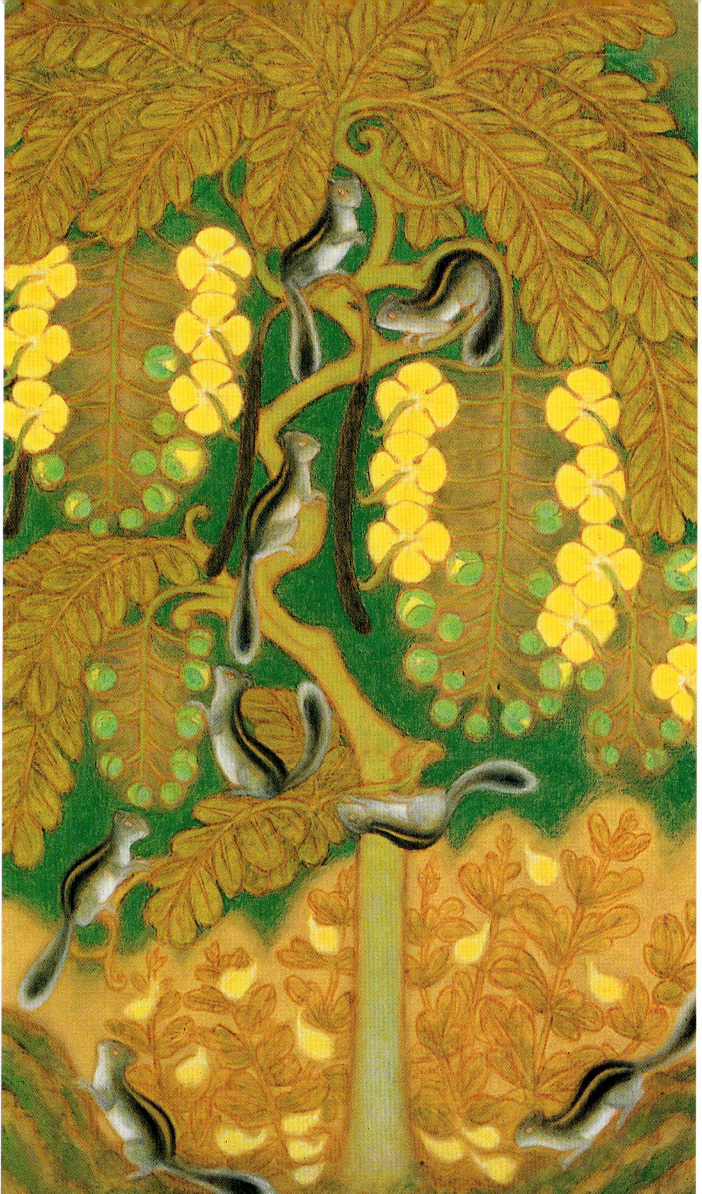

■ Squirrels on *amaltas* tree

Grey squirrels have appeared in details in Ramachandran's painted universe. In this painting, however, they are the centre of attention. The flowering amaltas *with its incandescent golden sprays of blossoms is a common feature of the Indian summer landscape. Here the twisted trunk of the tree creates its own pattern. The blossoms have just begun to open and the leaves are still young and coppery. Grey squirrels are scurrying along the branches. The browns, greys, yellows and greens indicate a different palette compared to the intense reds, blues, oranges and greens, generally seen in his oils. However, Ramachandran's palette shifts just as his reference points in traditional art change.* 4' x 2'8", oil on canvas, 1999.

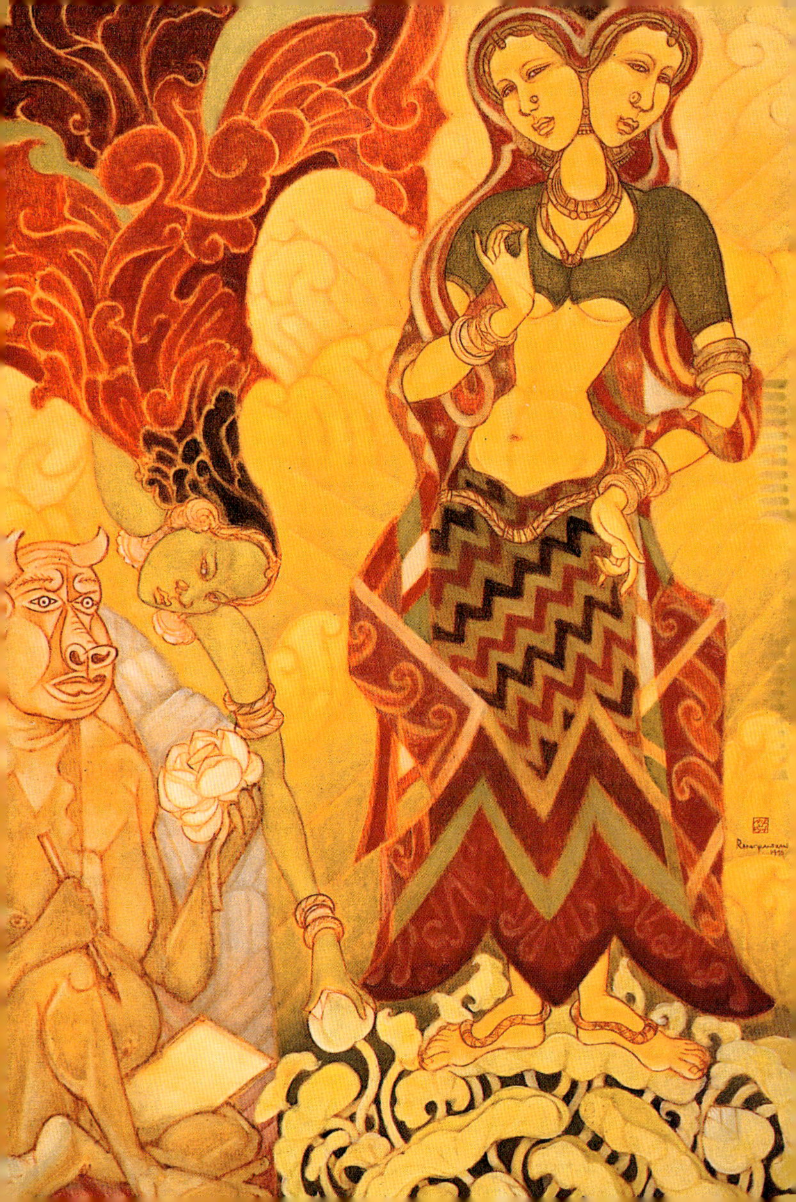

■ Urvashi and Minotaur

Urvashi, the heavenly apsara, *symbolises the muse whom the artist has been searching for all his life. He discovered her among the Bhils of Baneshwar. In the painting, he counterpoises her supple, willowy form bent slightly in* tribhanga *to capture the traditional Indian stance with Picasso's stocky Minotaur built up with fragmented planes. The arabesques in the background are similar in treatment to the sinuous forms of the lotuses in the foreground. The linear patterns of Urvashi's skirt are a counterpoint. Ramachandran seems to be contrasting the two notions of modernity in treatment between the west and the east.* 6'8" x 4'6", oil on canvas, 1990.

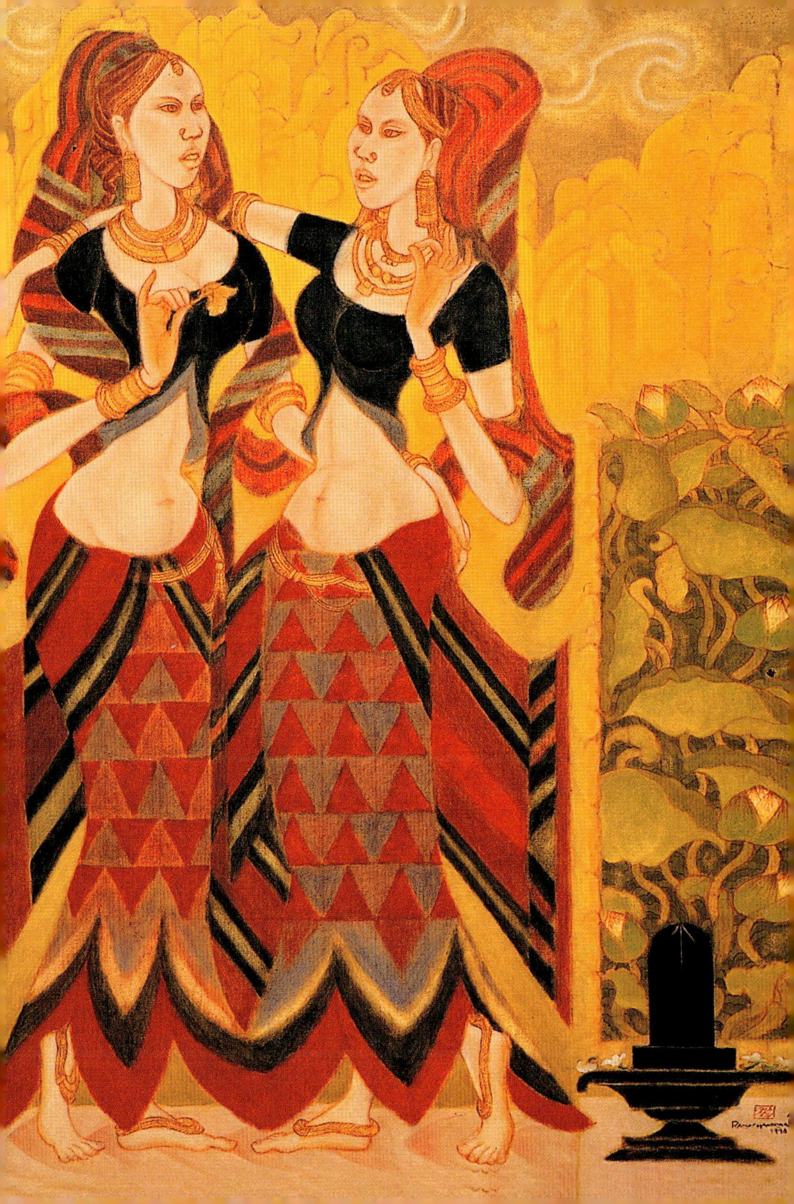

■ Urvashi at Baneshwar

Urvashi and her companion stand beside the Shivalinga. The figuration of the women, the design on textiles that they are wearing have been inspired by the Alchi monastery paintings at Ladakh. A panel of lotus flowers is on the right of the painting. The space division recalls the miniature tradition. Whether it is Ajanta or Sittanavasal, or Bundi and Pahari miniatures, or the works of the Santiniketan masters, the lotus ponds have many resonances for Ramachandran. The artist invests the paintings in the Urvashi series with a great deal of sensuousness. 6'8" x 4'6", oil on canvas, 1990.

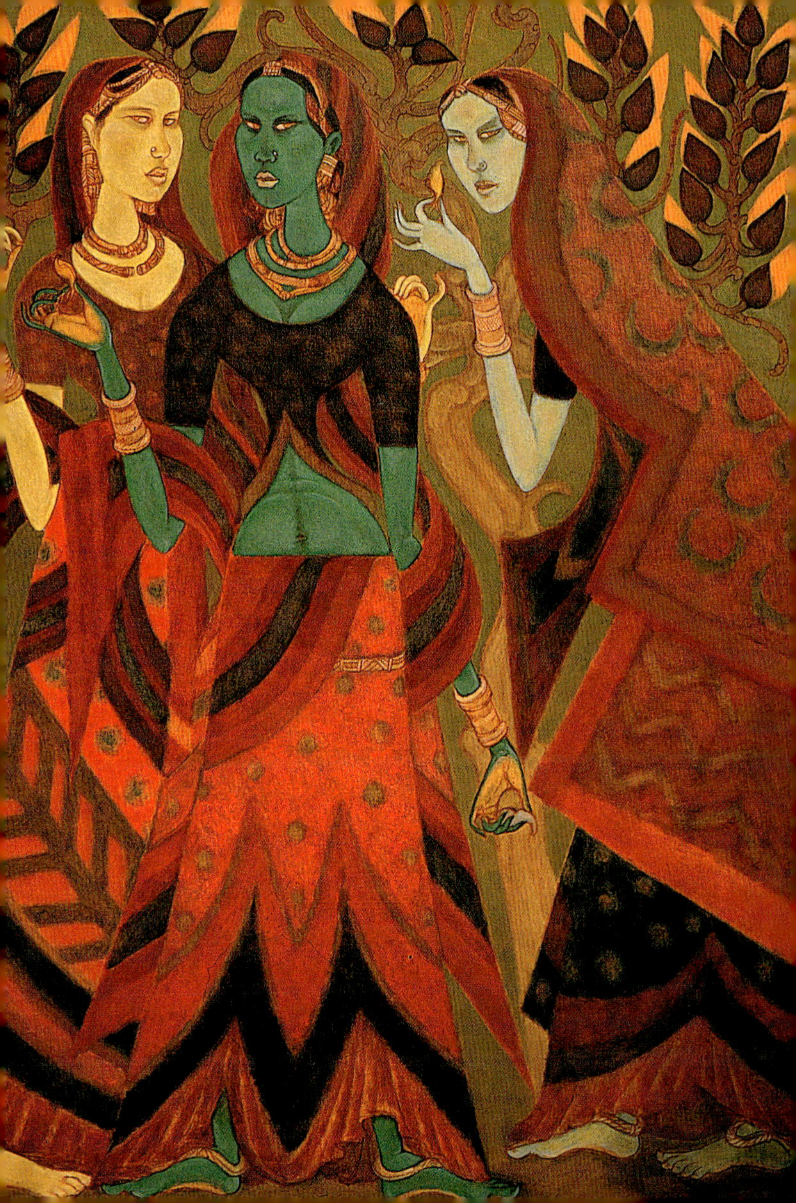

■ *Palash* tree and the tribal girls

As seen in the watercolours, the flaming palash *flower is a favourite motif of Ramachandran. In this painting, the flowering tree forms a suggestion of a backdrop. The elongated figures of the three tribal girls in their intricately patterned garments are placed in the foreground. Note the use of green in the complexion of the girl in the centre. The traditional word for it is* shyamal *and it is widely used in our texts and iconography. The treatment of the figures is akin to the 'Urvashi' series.* 6'8" x 4'8", oil on canvas, 1991.

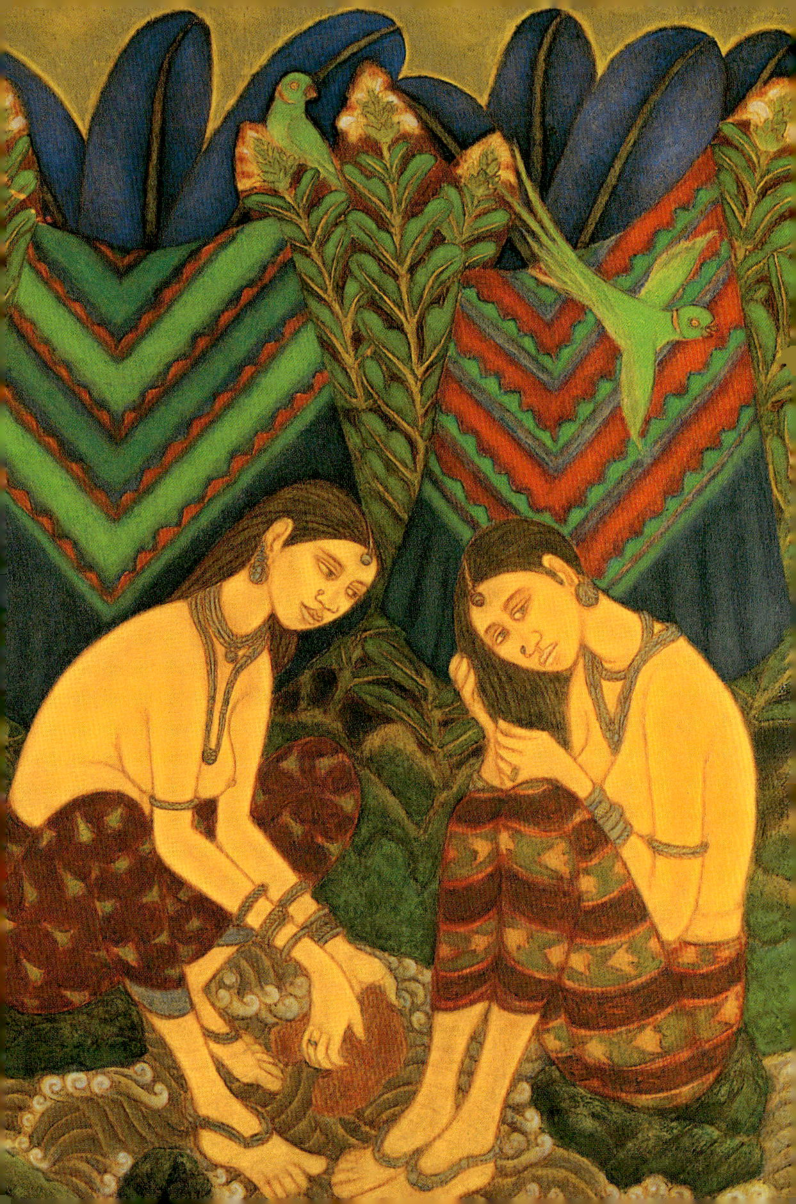

■ Bathers in the stream, Tutinama series

Ramchandran's Tutinama is different from the famous album of Mughal miniatures, just as his vision of the 'Squirrels on amaltas *tree' is radically distinct from the Mughal miniature 'Squirrels on a plane tree'. In the Tutinama of the Mughal emperors, a parrot narrates fascinating tales. Ramachandran's series is more visual in its starting point. Here the flight of parrots integrates the diverse paintings into a series. Bathers in the stream is a favourite motif in the artist's work. Here the blending of pattern and colours is worth savouring. Two women seated are bathing in a stream. Boldly striped garments tied to flowering shrubs are set out to dry. The flash of green and red of the flying parrot is an evocative counterpoint to the medley of colours.* 6'8" x 4'6", oil on canvas, 2000.

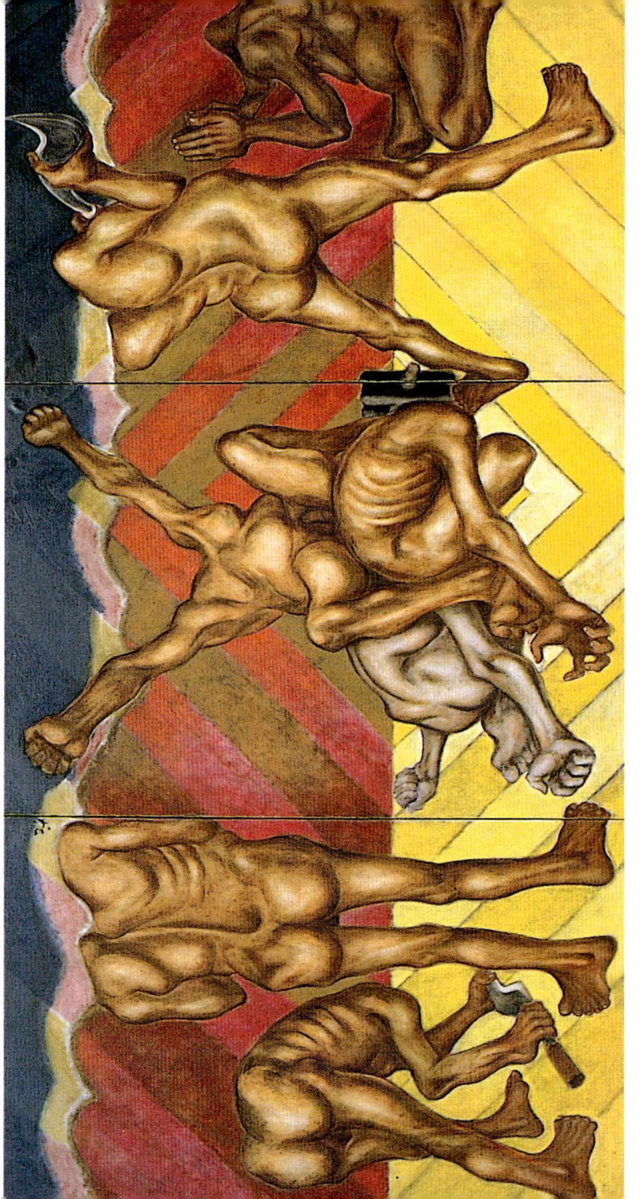

■ Kali Puja

This is an example of Ramachandran's earlier style of working. It was triggered off by a visit to Santiniketan in 1971. This was a period of great political unrest in West Bengal when the Naxalites rose up against the system and the government followed a policy of ruthless subjugation. It was a time of fear and anxiety for ordinary people. The headless figures in contorted stances, the sharpened sacrificial weapons and the menacing frame where the sacrifice is performed, all combine to express terror in the hearts of the people. 11'3" x 5'8", oil on canvas, 1972.

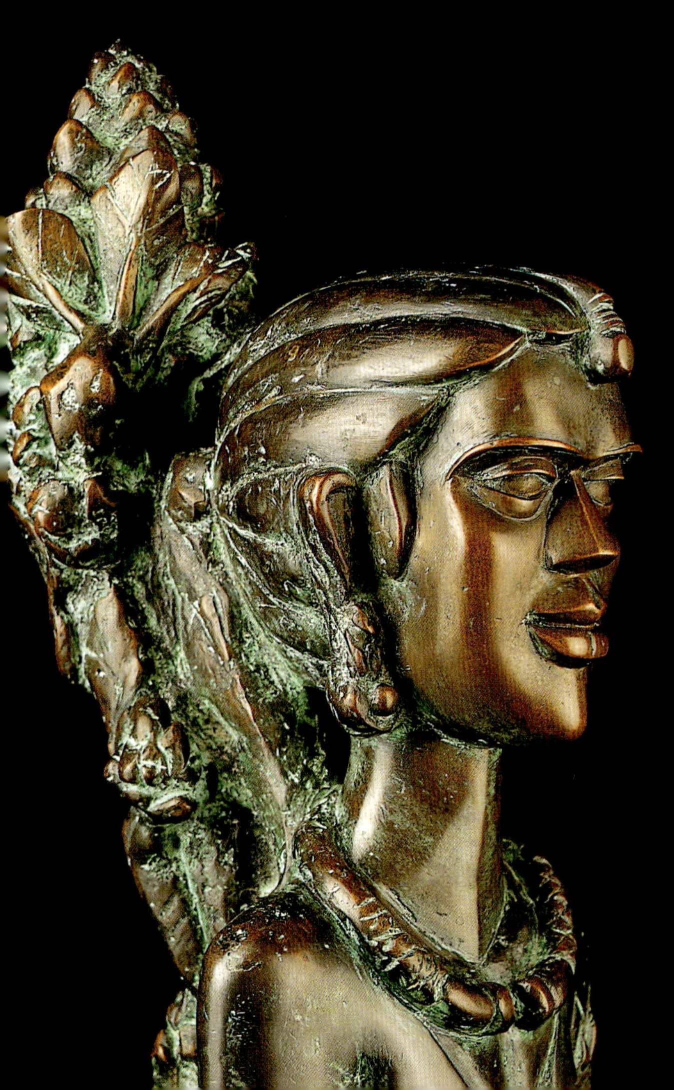

■ Basant: Roski with *palash* tree and chameleon, (detail)

During his Santiniketan days, Ramachandran trained in sculpture under Ramkinkar. It was not till 1982, however, that he took up sculpture in right earnest, although he had done occasional pieces earlier. In the Yayati series, he combined paintings and sculptures. The inspiration was his childhood memory of Kerala temples. It was in 1998 that he did a whole series of sculptures in which he expressed the closely integrated man-nature relationship that figured in his paintings since the early '80s. In these tall, narrow sculptures, forms are built upon each other and inextricably interrelated. The exuberant spirit of spring is depicted here. Ramachandran uses one of his favourite flora, the palash *tree. The tree and flowers are intricately linked to Roski's head so that they appear to form a part of the hairstyle.* 5'3", bronze, 1998.

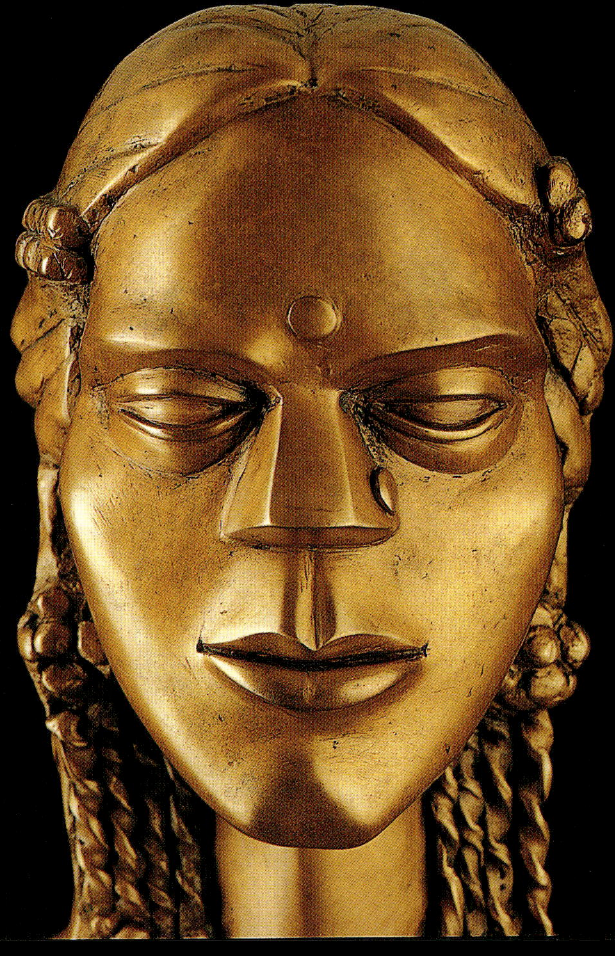

■ Bhav: Savita with *datura* plant and insects, (detail)

Savita, one of Dhowraji's daughters, is a favourite model for Ramachandran. In the unique set of sculptures executed in 1998, Ramachandran works out his philosophy of a closely integrated man-nature bond. The datura *plant puts Savita in a trance and clings to her closely. Just as in his paintings, in his sculptures too, Ramachandran creates a new iconography challenging the viewers with faces and forms found in the margin of the mainstream. Savita's face with her flattened nose, well-modelled lips and cleft chin surpasses the conventional notions of beauty. The whole sculpture has lush vegetation worked on the garments with bumble-bees resting on them. Savita stands on the artist's self-portrait as a mythical creature – a winged lion with a human face.* 5'7", bronze, 1998.

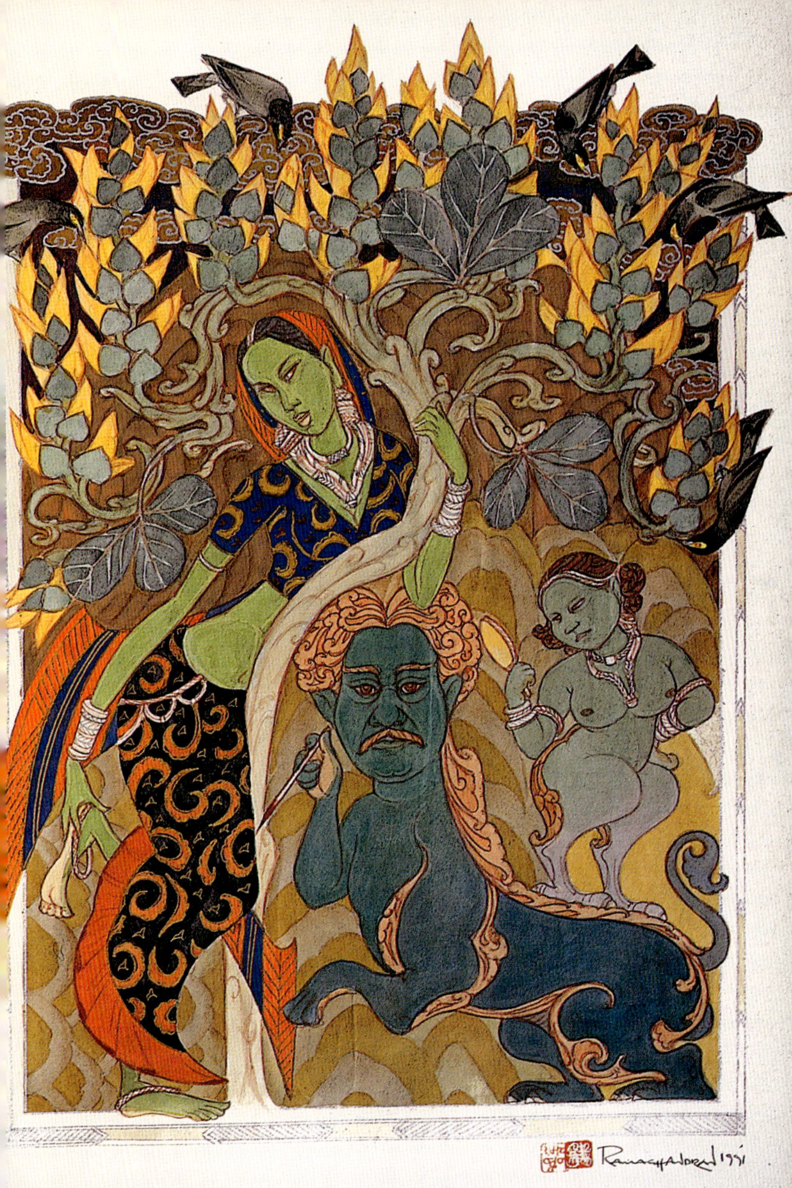

■ Myth of the *palash* tree

These watercolours were a part of the 'Reality in Search of a Myth' series. The artist always takes off from a point of reality to a realm of fantasy. A woman standing under a palash (Butea frondosa) *tree becomes a manifestation of luxuriant, teeming spirit of nature. In this beautiful scene, Ramachandran introduces himself as a man-lion. There is another creature – half-woman, half-fauna – holding a mirror, a favourite motif of the artist. The prolific birds on the tree heighten the elan and abundance that we encounter in nature. Note the lyrical, rhythmic lines repeated as in poetry. The form of a flame suggested by the shape of the flower is repeated all over.* 11.5" x 15.5", watercolour, 1992.

■ *Front cover:* Myth of the Palash tree II. 11.5" x 15.5", watercolour, 1992.